Big Cats

Jaguars

by Marie Brandle

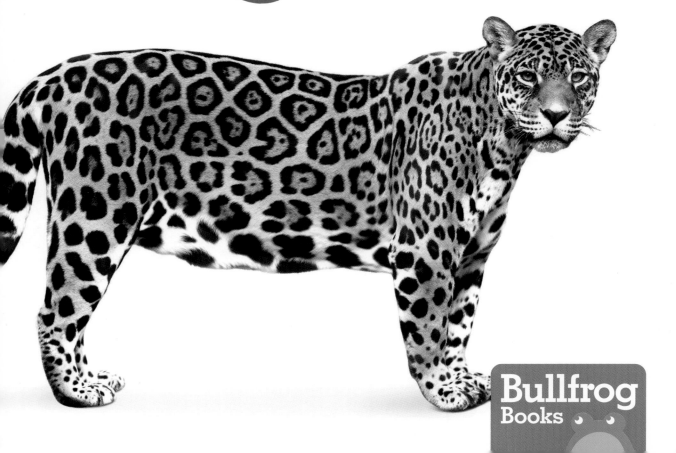

Bullfrog Books

Ideas for Parents and Teachers

Bullfrog Books let children practice reading informational text at the earliest reading levels. Repetition, familiar words, and photo labels support early readers.

Before Reading

- Discuss the cover photo. What does it tell them?

- Look at the picture glossary together. Read and discuss the words.

Read the Book

- "Walk" through the book and look at the photos. Let the child ask questions. Point out the photo labels.

- Read the book to the child, or have him or her read independently.

After Reading

- Prompt the child to think more. Ask: What did you know about jaguars before reading this book? What more would you like to learn about them?

Bullfrog Books are published by Jump!
5357 Penn Avenue South
Minneapolis, MN 55419
www.jumplibrary.com

Library of Congress Cataloging-in-Publication Data

Names: Brandle, Marie, 1989– author.
Title: Jaguars / by Marie Brandle.
Description: Minneapolis, MN: Jump!, Inc., [2021]
Series: Big cats | Includes index.
Audience: Ages 5–8 | Audience: Grades K–1
Identifiers: LCCN 2020023299 (print)
LCCN 2020023300 (ebook)
ISBN 9781645277217 (hardcover)
ISBN 9781645277224 (ebook)
Subjects: LCSH: Leopard—Juvenile literature.
Jaguar—Juvenile literature.
Classification: LCC QL737.C23 B7246 2021 (print)
LCC QL737.C23 (ebook) | DDC 599.75/5—dc23
LC record available at https://lccn.loc.gov/2020023299
LC ebook record available at https://lccn.loc.gov/2020023300

Editor: Eliza Leahy
Designer: Michelle Sonnek

Photo Credits: Anan Kaewkhammul/Shutterstock, cover; Martin Mecnarowski/Shutterstock, 1; Albertus Bonke/Shutterstock, 3; Dennis van de Water/Shutterstock, 4, 23bm; Pedro Helder Pinheiro/Shutterstock, 5; GUDKOV ANDREY/Shutterstock, 6–7, 8–9; Picture by Tambako the Jaguar/Getty, 10; bluehand/Shutterstock, 11; Kelp Grizzly Photography/Shutterstock, 12–13, 23br; Hans Wagemaker/Shutterstock, 14–15; Adalbert Dragon/Shutterstock, 16–17; Wonderly Imaging/Shutterstock, 18, 23tm; gerard lacz/Alamy, 19, 23tr; ZSSD/Minden Pictures/SuperStock, 20–21, 23tl; Ursula Pinheiro/Shutterstock, 23bl; Ana Vasileva/Shutterstock, 24.

Printed in the United States of America at Corporate Graphics in North Mankato, Minnesota.

Table of Contents

Dark Spots

It is hot in the rain forest.

A jaguar sleeps high in a tree.

Jaguars are big cats.
Their fur is tan.
They have dark spots.

spot

Their fur helps them hide.
Cool!

Their claws are sharp.

claw ....▶

10

Claws help them climb.
Jaguars rest on branches.
Neat!

They scratch trees.
Why?

It leaves a scent.

Other jaguars smell it.

They stay away.

This jaguar swims.
Why?
It hunts for prey.

tooth

Jaguars have big teeth.
They are sharp!

This mom goes to her den.
Her cubs are inside!

den ····▶

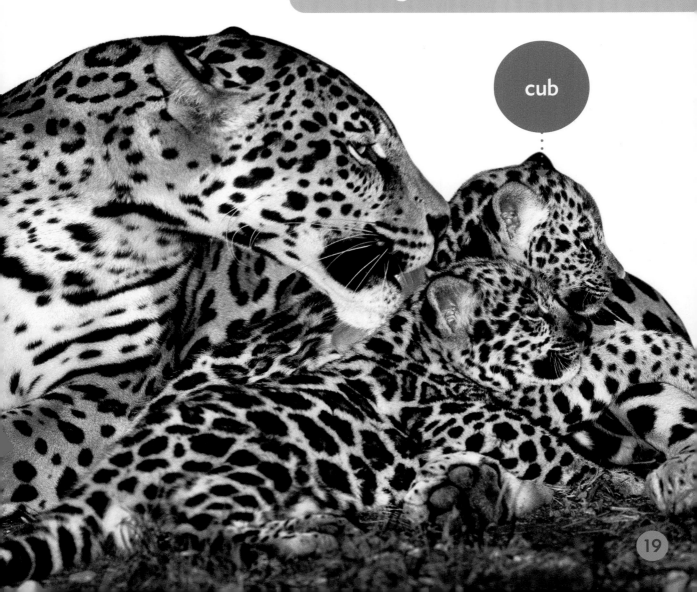

She grooms them.

cub

She will teach
them to hunt.

For now, they play!

Where in the World?

Most jaguars live in rain forests in South America and North America. Take a look!

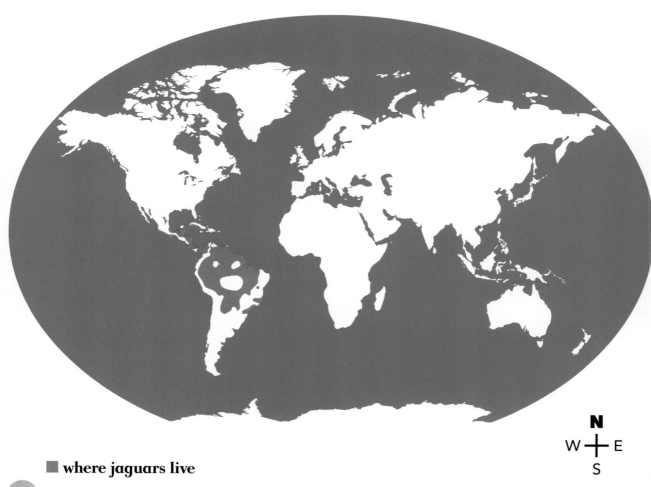

■ where jaguars live

Picture Glossary

cubs
Young jaguars.

den
The home of
a wild animal.

grooms
Cleans. A jaguar
mother grooms
her cubs by licking
their fur.

prey
An animal that is
hunted by another
animal for food.

rain forest
A dense, tropical
forest where a
lot of rain falls
throughout the year.

scent
The odor of
an animal.

Index

To Learn More

FACT SURFER

Finding more information is as easy as 1, 2, 3.

❶ Go to www.factsurfer.com

❷ Enter "jaguars" into the search box.

❸ Choose your book to see a list of websites.